C. 2

J
599.74

MacClintock, Dorcus
Phoebe the
kinkajou

DATE DUE

FEB 1 9 1987			
APR 2 9 1987			
APR 1 5 1994			
DEC 0 3 1996			
OCT 1 7 1997			

PHOEBE
THE
KINKAJOU

Phoebe the Kinkajou

by Dorcas MacClintock

photographs by Ellan Young

CHARLES SCRIBNER'S SONS • NEW YORK

Library of Congress Cataloging in Publication Data

MacClintock, Dorcas.   Phoebe the Kinkajou.
   Bibliography: p.
   Includes index.
   Summary: Follows a kinkajou from her home in a tropical forest to her new life as a
pet in an American household and describes the characteristics and behavior of these
animals in general.
   1. Kinkajou—Juvenile literature.
2. Kinkajou—Biography—Juvenile literature.
3. Kinkajou as pets—Juvenile literature.   [1. Kinkajou]
I. Young, Ellan, ill.   II. Title.
QL737.C26M335   1985   599.74'443   85-10823
ISBN 0-684-18310-2

Photo credits: pages 5, 6, 28, Andrew Young; pages 10, 29 (top),
Deedra McClearn; page 70, Ivo Poglayen. Drawing on page 54 of
Phoebe by Charles Gentry from Jenkins and McClearn, *Journal of
Morphology* 182 (1984): 199.

"THE KINKAJOU" lyric on page 50 by Joseph McCarthy, music by
Harry Tierney © 1926, renewed 1954 LEO FEIST INC. Rights
assigned to CBS CATALOGUE PARTNERSHIP. All rights controlled and
administered by CBS FEIST CATALOG INC. All rights reserved.
International copyright secured. Used by permission.

To Deedra McClearn and Andrew Young
Phoebe's accomplices and ours

CONTENTS

Phoebe

In the shadowy darkness, high on a shelf, soft sounds and muffled stirrings come from inside a large basket. Phoebe the kinkajou is waking. Unless she is routed out of her basket or frightened, waking is a slow process.

After several minutes, Phoebe's mantled head pushes up. Large eyes, topped by soft, buff-yellow brows, give a gentle expression to her round brown face. Small half-circle ears are set low on the sides of her head. The gently pointed muzzle is partly covered with crumpled vibrissae, or whiskers. The brown rhinarium, or nose pad, is deeply grooved.

Phoebe disappears under the covers, adjusting them over and around her curved form with forepaw pulls, teeth tugs, and nose nudges.

Minutes later, Phoebe emerges. About the size of a house cat, but longer and slimmer-bodied, she has a tail nearly as long as her head and body. Her powerful head-trunk musculature is so loosely covered by her skin that along the belly her plush fur forms folds. Phoebe is yellowish brown. Her fur has a bronze sheen. Dark brown marks her head and shoulders, extends down the front of her arms, covers her forepaws, and emphasizes the end of her tail. Her throat and belly are an incredible rich golden-orange color.

Phoebe the kinkajou once lived in the tropical forest. Much of the time she lived by herself, but sometimes she joined other kinkajous to feed and frolic in the trees.

The Tropical Forest

Phoebe's natural *habitat,** the tropical forest, is a wet and warm place. Tall tree trunks rise straight to disappear in a canopy of green leaves high overhead. Thin triangular plates called "buttresses" radiate for support from the trunks of some of the big trees. *Lianas* climb tree trunks and loop down from the canopy. They extend in twists and tangles from tree to tree. *Epiphytes,* or air plants, perch on high branches or grow in tree-trunk bark crevices. Many of them are *bromeliads,* relatives of the pineapple. Others are orchids and small ferns. Brightly colored blossoms—red, yellow, and blue—are high in the canopy. Except for fallen petals, the forest floor is muted in various shades of brown. Here and there in the dim light, seedlings sprout and ferns and dwarf palms grow. Where a giant tree has toppled, leaving a gap in the canopy, a tangled thicket grows in response to sunlight.

Phoebe had a favorite tree in the forest, a big almendro. Its huge columnar trunk was smooth-barked and difficult for an animal to climb. But Phoebe's route into and out of the tree was always through the canopy. The almendro's branches reached 100 feet and more above the forest floor. Around its base grew smaller trees, most of them limbless, with compact leaf crowns. Palms and saplings formed the understory, a place Phoebe seldom came down to explore.

---

*Italicized words are explained in the glossary (page 78).

4

Often there were other kinkajous in the almendro. And sometimes they were joined by small, owlish night monkeys with round heads and enormous staring eyes.

Within the forest, temperature and humidity are relatively constant. Air temperature ranges between 70 and 90°F (21 and 32°C). Occasionally, during the rainy season, it dips into the low 60s, or in dry months climbs to 95°F. Humidity ranges from a dry-season 75 to 80 percent to 91 to 95 percent in the wet months.

Under constant high temperature and humidity, processes of decay are rapid. Ants, termites, beetles, millipedes, and bacteria work tirelessly to break down leaves, petals, and fruits that fall to the ground.

6

Their waste products furnish nutrients that are readily absorbed by plants.

Beneath the thin leaf litter are fungi. Dependent upon the trees as sources of energy, their white threads interweave with tiny tree rootlets and recycle phosphorus and potassium, minerals essential to tree growth.

The soil supports an array of plant species. Although the number of individual animals in the tropical forest may be relatively small, the number of animal species is large. Differences in feeding times (night or day), diet (fruit, leaves, or insects and other animals), and foraging levels (canopy, understory, or on the ground) reduce competition for food and enable these species to share the forest.

When it is very hot and humid, Phoebe leaves her basket and lies stretched out and draped on a branch or shelf. On hottest days, when the air is still and oppressive, she has a fan. Then she moves to the shelf over the open door and dips forepaws and hind feet into its cooling air current.

The Rainstorm

Rainstorms in the tropical forest sometimes are accompanied by spectacular displays of lightning and violent clashes of thunder. Perhaps this is why Phoebe, late one summer night, became so restive.

The day had been hot and humid. Just as a kinkajou in the forest would leave its tree-hollow den to spend such a day on a limb or atop a tangle of vines, Phoebe left her basket to drape her long body on a wide branch. Resting her head on one side, she closed her eyes and tried to sleep. She kept a loose tail wrap on the branch; her forelimbs and hind legs hung down. Smooth-skinned palms and soles, moist with sweat, were exposed for evaporative cooling.

Phoebe was slower than usual to wake that evening. Her people had not yet thought of recycling her time of activity, so dusk was waking time. She sprawled on her feeding shelf, showing little interest in checking the contents of her food plate. Eventually she picked up a few banana slices. These seemed to suffice for a hot-evening meal.

By nine o'clock Phoebe was active, alternating runs around her habitat with pauses to feed or to drape and pant. Two hours later, after her people had gone to bed, she made a few extra-fast circuits, exhaled explosively, then paused as though listening for a reply. She climbed onto the door top, then descended headfirst to the doorknob, and dropped forefeet-first onto the rug. She padded over to the bed, pulled

herself up, and pushed an inquisitive, soft-whiskered, moist muzzle against one and then the other sleeping form. Then she settled in a curl between them. But not for long.

Flashes of lightning lit the room. Thunder sounded. Wind from the west was tossing treetops and blowing in the windows.

With a tail wrap around a sleeper's lower leg, Phoebe let herself down over the side of the bed. Noiselessly she padded out into the hall, peered in a bathroom, then turned left. She startled the big red cat, sleep-

24

ing beneath the highboy. But Phoebe didn't wait for his reaction. She explored the guest room, then down the stairs, her long, thin body as sinuous as a snake's. She checked the living room, the hall, and the study, casting about at her relentless bowlegged trot. Through the dining room she went and into the kitchen.

BJ, the orphan baby blue jay, head tucked under a newly feathered wing and fast asleep, occupied the below-the-counter cage that had been Phoebe's place when she arrived. Phoebe paid no attention, and the small fledgling bird went on sleeping. She bounded up the steep backstairs to the studio. There was Mike the cat, asleep on a sculpture stand. He looked down, yawned.

Phoebe found that her usual return route through the big back closet into the bedroom and her own habitat was closed off. Wind had banged the door shut. In a panic, she dashed down the back stairs. She trotted through the dining room, raced up the front stairs, and onto the bed.

Flashes of lightning and claps of thunder came almost at the same time. The downpour of rain blew in the west window. Surely her people should share in the excitement. Phoebe stood tall on her haunches, then launched a mock attack. A knee, then a foot, a wrist, then an elbow. They quickly woke up.

After a short tussle and unsuccessful attempts to smother the kinkajou under the covers, they carried Phoebe back to her quarters. For the rest of the night she enjoyed the cool air that came in her window and her people went back to sleep.

Being Nocturnal

Phoebe's preference for the dark is evident. She is more strongly nocturnal than a raccoon, which is to say she restricts her activity to darkness. Raccoons, where they feel safe, often forage in the dim light of dusk and dawn.

The reasons for the kinkajou's choice of night life can be speculated. In the tropical forest, nighttime canopy competitors, such as bats and night monkeys, are never as numerous as their daytime counterparts: troops of lively little monkeys called capuchins, howler monkeys, and

spider monkeys, bands of coatis, and fruit-eating birds. Darkness also provides better protection from *predators;* the weasel-like tayra, the gray fox, the jaguarundi, and two climbing cats, the jaguar and a small spotted cat called the margay.

Kinkajous often move through the branches and feed in the company of night-monkey families and sometimes olingos.* When there is little or no moonlight, a system of mutual avoidance prevails. On moonlight nights, activity peaks and the animals race up and down vines and through tree branches. On any night, the silent swoop of an owl or the coiled ambush of a boa constrictor can put an end to their frolic.

Night travel in the treetops requires a familiarity with pathways that involves memory. Kinkajous, like all animals, are creatures of habit. And they have retentive memories. Each individual, or group of individuals, relies on an intimate knowledge, gained through the senses, of a *home range*. Kinkajou home ranges are overlapping. Within the confines of the home range, a kinkajou moves about almost automatically and knows where denning or safe resting places are and where food is to be found. It recognizes kinkajou neighbors. And it knows what routes to take to elude or flee from a predator.

---

*The olingo, a look-alike relative of the kinkajou, has a long, faintly banded, nonprehensile tail.

Phoebe and Her Senses

Nocturnal mammals rely on the sense of touch and on the sense of smell. Many of them have secreting glands and ritualized patterns of marking behavior. Secretions used in olfactory communication, called *pheromones,* are reliable chemical signals that transmit in darkness and last for days.

Scent-marking behavior, common among procyonids, is highly developed in the kinkajou. In the tropical forest, home ranges are defined by scent marking, and travel routes are established along branches and vines. Scent marking, a means of maintaining social organization, enables a kinkajou to make or avoid contact with another of its species.

Even in captivity, given a large enough enclosure, a kinkajou scent marks. Conspicuous on either side of Phoebe's face, at the corners of her mouth, are bare areas. These are her paired mandibular (or jaw) glands.

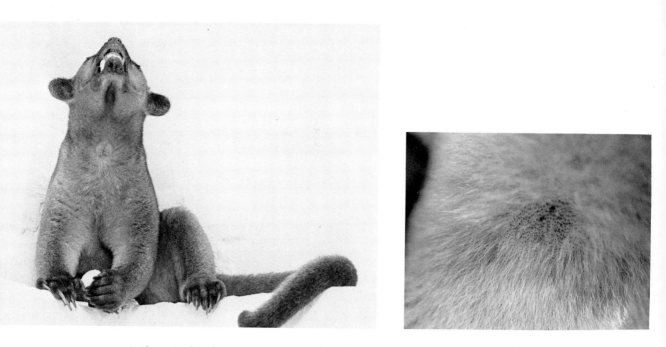

A throat gland appears as another bare patch, as does an abdominal gland. Phoebe has a sweet, musklike odor that probably is associated with secretions from these glands. It may be that the secretions of each of the three glands mean different things to other kinkajous.

Phoebe uses her mandibular glands to mark people, with a gesture that is something like a cat's brief facial greeting. She also marks door tops and branch tips. Throat and abdominal glands are used to mark larger objects and favorite resting places on branches and shelves.

The high tramway that extends around the upper perimeter of Phoebe's room becomes layered with dark brown *sebum* (a fatty secretion of scent-marking skin glands) and dirt. Every few weeks it is scrubbed clean, a process that provides Phoebe renewed incentive to scent mark.

Being a nocturnal forest dweller, Phoebe relies more on hearing than on sight. Acoustic signals are flexible, varying from barely audible soft sounds to loud screams. They also have a greater reach than scent-gland signals.

Phoebe can be very vocal. During her sleeping hours she makes only occasional sounds, sleepy stirrings sometimes punctuated by a soft moan. When she is active, she sometimes makes a high-pitched sound that is her short-range contact call, a plaintive, whistling *kwit, kwit*. Its energy quickly dissipates in the air. In the forest, scattered by canopy leaves and branches, the call would not carry far.

When Phoebe is active, she often puffs as she strides vigorously overhead. Sometimes this explosive exhaling precedes a barking that is her medium-range contact call.

The air fills with noise—squeaks, hisses, barks, and *wook* calls—on full-moon nights when night monkeys join kinkajous in a fruit-laden tree. There are frequent, brief-but-vocal displays of threat or anger between kinkajou and kinkajou and between kinkajou and night monkey.

A loose *commensal* relation may exist between kinkajous and night monkeys, one species being benefited, the other neither benefited nor harmed. Home ranges of the two species are overlapping, and both animals feed on the same kinds of fruits and insects, searching through the night for these patchily distributed food sources. The similarity of their contact calls suggests that they may rely on each other to locate feeding sites.

Occasionally, after a bout of excited, high-speed racing, Phoebe emits a shrill, quavering scream, a usually repeated, low-pitched call that would carry far in the forest.

When Phoebe visited a wildlife photographer's studio to be included in a film on tropical animals, her camera time on the large, down-curved limb came immediately after the filming of a six-foot-long boa constrictor. Prevented from seeing the boa before her turn on the branch, Phoebe did not appear to detect the potential predator by smell. But a kinkajou's hearing is keen. In the forest Phoebe undoubtedly would have been alerted by the sound of the snake's curving body as it moved along a limb or by the vibration of a branch. Rustling sounds—of leaves or of rumpled sheets of newspapers—always cause Phoebe to race around her tramway in obvious agitation.

Phoebe, like many nocturnal animals, has round, relatively large eyes. For efficient night vision the cornea bulges and even protrudes, and the lens is large, so that Phoebe's eyes gather as much of the available night light as possible. The pupil also is large and round, its aperture size controlled by a chestnut-brown iris. The *tapetum,* a glistening layer of opaque tissue at the back of the eye, functions as a mirror, reflecting stray light back through the retina to give it a second chance to stimulate one of the visual cells. When Phoebe peers out from her dark room into the well-lighted hall or when she looks into the beam of a flashlight, her eyes shine yellow, sometimes orange, as reflected light shines back through the lenses.

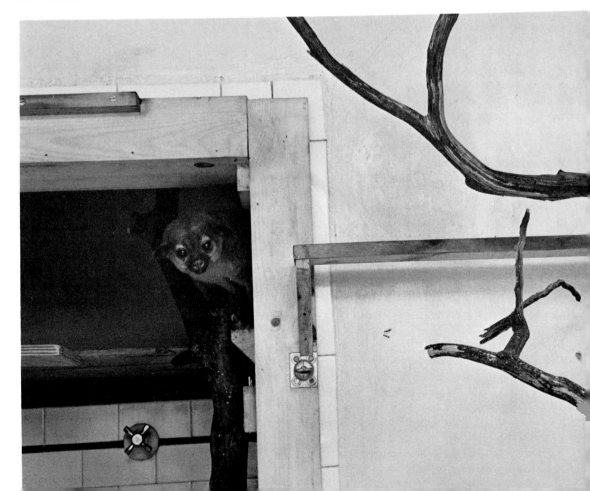

The retina itself is filled with rod cells. Rods and cones are the two kinds of retinal sense cells. Rods function in dim-light perception, distinguishing differences in brightness and rather blurry images. They are of more use in night vision than are cone cells, used for bright-light discernment of detail and for color perception. The retinas of some nocturnal animals' eyes have no cones. Phoebe's retina probably has some cones, but it is likely that she, like most of the *carnivores* (members of the mammalian order Carnivora), perceives differences in brightness rather than actual colors.

Phoebe's eyes are set well to the front of her head, which is to say, she has orbits, or eye sockets, that are convergent, allowing for overlap of visual fields. Orbital convergence is sometimes regarded as an adaptation for gauging distance when the animal leaps from branch to branch, but it is also seen in slow-moving primates like the lorises and in a rather stodgy marsupial called the spotted cuscus. Tree squirrels, the ultimate acrobats, have laterally placed eyes. So the correlation between orbital convergence and arboreal athletics is questionable.

Orbital convergence probably relates to predation. Owls, hawks, and cats depend upon visual overlap in capturing swift and often elusive prey. So does a kinkajou when it strikes or snatches an insect or other small animal.

Brownish fur color, like Phoebe's, is common among humid-forest mammals. While light from the night sky is bluish, the forest canopy mostly lets in light at the red end of the spectrum, to which nocturnal mammals are relatively insensitive. Thus the forest becomes a dark-red world in which the body outlines of reddish-brown and yellowish-brown animals are difficult to discern.

Phoebe has a delicate sense of touch, even though her forepaws resemble those of the giant panda or a bear more than they do the delicate, long-fingered forepaws of a raccoon. For a third of their lengths Phoebe's fingers and toes are webbed, but her bare-skinned palms are well supplied with sensory nerve endings. Of the tropical forest's canopy animals, only the little night monkey, with its dextrous hands, is better equipped than a kinkajou for probing in tree crannies.

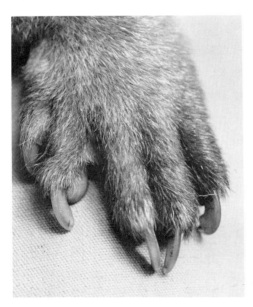

In 1865, J. E. Gray watched a London Zoo kinkajou feeding. It held the bread in one hand and with the other pulled off small pieces and put them in its mouth. This, the zoologist noted, it did "like a small child and quite as handily."

Phoebe uses her forepaws when eating. A fresh fig is grasped between her hands, even when she hangs by hind feet and tail, and consumed. A marshmallow is taken in one hand, while she pulls off piece after sticky piece with her teeth. If she is given a marshmallow in her basket, she clutches the donor's finger with her free hand.

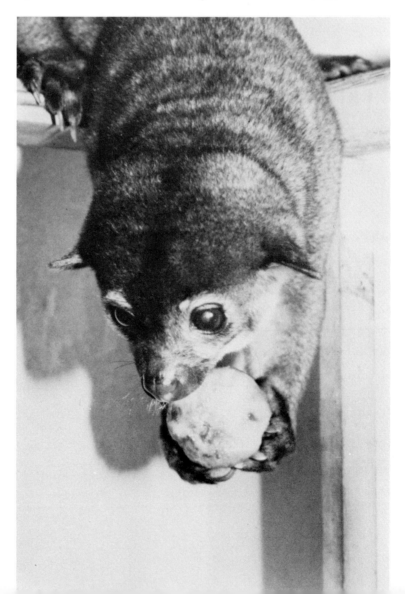

Experiments carried out by German psychologists Rensch and Dücker indicate that a kinkajou has considerable manipulative ability. Their kinkajou learned to open seven different closures on two boxes, one nested inside the other. After pushing aside an outer board, the kinkajou opened a hook, pushed back a padlock bar, pressed a lever to open a sliding door, and then pushed the door to one side. Then the kinkajou pulled on a wooden ball to open a third sliding door, which it pushed up. Finally it removed a cover from the aluminum dish to find its food reward.

This kinkajou also exhibited learning retention. After 172 days away from the boxes, it returned to open the seven baffles in about 15 seconds.

When leaving one branch for another, a kinkajou proceeds with caution. Grasping hands and feet are essential for this maneuver. Like many arboreal mammals, Phoebe has hind feet that are more specialized for prehension (holding on) than are her forepaws. With a firm hind-end attachment, hind feet gripping and tail wrapped about one branch, she crosses over to the other branch.

Mishaps are rare, but Robert K. Enders, observing kinkajous on Barro Colorado Island, saw one female catch herself just in time. When her hind feet, secured on slim twigs, failed to hold her, the kinkajou clamped her tail on the branch itself. This brought her up with a jerk. Then she reached for a twig on the next tree, carefully pulled the branch to her, and made her way across.

42

Phoebe delights in hanging head down from limb, tramway, or doorframe. Her body swings freely from ankles and tail. Her head turns this way and that as she peers out into the room. After a few seconds or several minutes, she loops herself back up onto her perch and resumes locomoting or descends the tree trunk to explore the house.

Tails that are used for balance, important to fast-moving arboreal animals, tend to be long. Night monkeys rely on their long, heavily furred tail as a counterbalance. Phoebe, too, uses her tail to maintain balance. As she hurtles around the narrow overhead track in her room, her tail—carried with an upward loop that is down-curved at the end—swings to the inside of the track as she anticipates the sharp corners. Long, rounded, and evenly furred, her tail consists of 29 vertebrae. Except for those at the tip, the vertebrae have conspicuous bony projections for attachment of the tail's powerful muscles.

44

While some feeding is done within a tree's dense crown, often a kinkajou must feed on spikes or panicles or seed-containing pods that grow on tips of slender branches. Then balance, careful footwork, and the strong *prehensile* tail are important. The kinkajou climbs out to the tips of branches to bite off and eat fruits. With hind foot and tail support, it extends a forepaw and pulls a fruit-laden branch within feeding range. Tail grip is also employed when a kinkajou reaches high over its head or stretches its long body from one limb to another.

45

On a narrow ledge Phoebe presses her body against the wall. On a half-inch of corner molding, she relies on a mountain-climbing technique. With hind feet secured, she pushes her back against the wall. Her tail serves as a prop as her upper body swings around for a change of direction.

46

Prehensile tails are common in South America, where all kinds of mammals have independently developed them. An arboreal porcupine has a prehensile tail. So has one of the anteaters. Several of the marsupials have prehensile tails, and monkeys depend upon their grasping tails. But the kinkajou is the only carnivore that has a prehensile tail.*

---

*In southern Asia an arboreal carnivore called the binturong has a tail that is prehensile, but only at the tip.

Essentially a fifth limb, the muscular tail is also useful when Phoebe hangs from door tops or brakes on a steep descent. Without the security of its grip, a kinkajou would have to rely, as squirrels often do, on hind-foot claws. Even for a smaller animal like the squirrel, this is precarious. While kinkajous, with their grasping tails, can feed aloft, squirrels nip off the nut- or seed-bearing tips of branches and then must scamper down the trunk to retrieve and gnaw on them.

48

Phoebe has the forearm mobility of all good climbers. Her *scapula* (shoulder blade) is set high on her rib cage. She has forepaws that are *palmigrade* (the bare-skinned palms contact the branch) and hind feet that are *semiplantigrade* (not quite flat-footed). Fur extends well below the ankles. On bare soles she pads along branches.

As Phoebe strides along the bannister, it is easy to see that she is bowlegged. All kinkajous are bowlegged. She swings each short, stout forelimb out in a lateral arc, with little flexion, much as a sailor swings his legs in a rolling gait on the deck of a heaving ship. Forepaws are set down on the outside of the palm. This way of locomoting accommodates the rounded contour of branch or bannister. It also facilitates her rapid reaction and quick correction movements in case of loss of balance or a slip.

Phoebe's trot is relentless. Around and around she goes on the over-head tramway in her room. Her rapid footfalls always trace the same pattern through the branches of her tree. Going downstairs (or coming back up) Phoebe is sinuous. Her long body and trailing tail form moving S-curves.

A South American dance rhythm of the 1930s celebrates this smooth way of moving. From the romantic musical comedy *Rio Rita*, with words by Joseph McCarthy, the song is called "The Kinkajou":

> When you do the Kinkajou,
> You'll dance before you think you do. . . .
> You clown around, you're feeling, oh so lazy,
> 'Fore you know you're shouting "Whoops a daisy". . . .

Once downstairs, Phoebe trots purposefully from room to room. Now and again she breaks into a half-bounding gallop. Her hind feet give thrust, and her forefeet touch down with a close one-two beat, the second forefoot reaching ahead of the first. Her long spine humps as hind feet are carried forward to touch down just after the forefeet begin another stride.

Accomplished aerialists that they are, kinkajous make lemurlike leaps through the branches of a tree, with their bodies nearly upright. Phoebe, being housebound, leaps over sleeping dogs, cats, off the banister, or down the tree trunk in her room. She pushes off with her hind feet and absorbs landing impact with her forefeet. A soft *ker-plunk* announces a kinkajou on the loose.

When Deedra McClearn returned to the Museum of Comparative Zoology at Harvard University with Phoebe, her research focused on Phoebe's ankle, the joint that enables a kinkajou to descend tree trunk or vine headfirst (rather than backing down as a domestic cat does) and to hang upside down like an acrobat. Radiographs were made of Phoebe's hind feet as she ran on a small treadmill in the laboratory, as she climbed up or down, or hung from a horizontal branch.

The ankle joint in mammals is composed of seven bones. Two are larger than the others: the calcaneus, which projects backward as the heel, and the talus, which articulates with the bones of the lower leg (tibia and fibula). A small, curved navicular bone is just in front of the talus. In front of the calcaneus is the cuboid, an elongated little bone aligned with the three small, squarish cuneiform bones.

In most mammals the ankle bones are fairly stable. Ankle movement is restricted, to greater or lesser degree, to a fore-and-aft plane, with only some lateral rotation. Phoebe, however, is swivel footed.

A look at the human ankle, flexible as it is, makes swiveling a foot seem an impossible feat. Yet for Phoebe and a few other arboreal animals*, ankles are made for rotation. These animals can rotate their hind feet out and (to varying degrees) turn them backwards, so that *plantar* surfaces and clawed digits, or toes, become effective hanging devices.

Hind-foot rotation is accomplished in different ways. The opossum hind foot inverts at the joint between tibia and talus, with outward rotation also occurring at knee and hip. Deedra McClearn and Farish A. Jenkins, Jr., her major professor, found that in procyonids, hind-foot reversal, or *inversion*, is achieved at different joints. Raccoon and coati, Phoebe's climbing relatives, exhibit some movement at the *subtalar joint*

_____

*Squirrels, tree shrews, some primitive primates, the procyonids, the viverrids (a group of Old World carnivores), the margay, and the opossum.

(as the calcaneus slides forward, rotating under the talus) and at the *transverse tarsal joint* (between calcaneus and talus and the navicular-cuboid area). There is also some rotation in the hip joint. But the grasping hind feet of the raccoon and the coati are never fully reversed when they descend tree or vine headfirst.

When Phoebe swivels her hind foot (which she can rotate out through 180 degrees), there is increased movement—up to 90 degrees—at each of the two joints, subtalar and transverse tarsal. No out-turning occurs at the hip, knee, or tibiotarsal joints. With claws and footpads

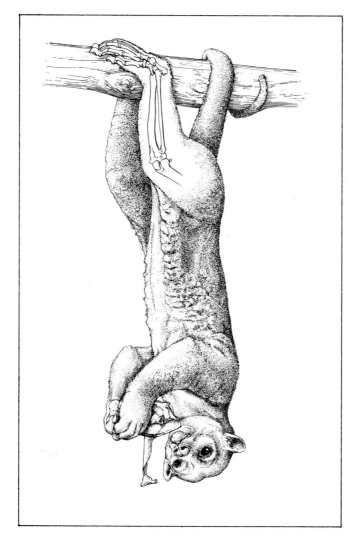

reversed, she has no problem descending a vertical trunk headfirst or hanging upside down, even by one hind foot. Her method of hind-foot inversion—much like that of another superb gymnast, the gray squirrel—allows her to enjoy just hanging.

Food for a Kinkajou

In the tropics, where fruit is available year-round, frugivory (fruit eating) is a way of life, even among the carnivores. Some mammals are fruit eaters in part, others are full-time frugivores. Some have preferences for certain fruits, others are generalists and eat many kinds of fruits.

A kinkajou's monkeylike skull, short and round with a convex frontal region, has 36 teeth, all well suited for eating fruit. The incisors, neat rows of close-meeting chisel-like nippers, are used to bite off fruit. The canines, long, grooved, and sharply pointed, are good for holding grape-sized fruit in the mouth. The premolars have small bladelike cutting

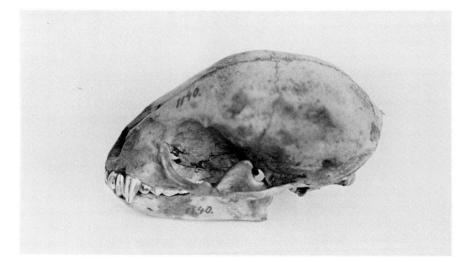

cusps. The molars are broad, flat crushing teeth.

These teeth are also effective for chewing flesh. Phoebe, like all procyonids, is an opportunist. She eats what is available. Therefore she is termed a frugivore-*omnivore*. While much of her diet consists of fruit, she also eats animal food.

Kinkajous relish night-swarming insects as well as those found on tree trunks and leaves. They feed on tree-living frogs, small amphibians whose chorus of croaks and *tonks* fills the night forest. They pilfer eggs, devour nestlings, and occasionally kill roosting birds.

For Phoebe, *protein* comes in two favorite foods: eggs and smelts. The small fish (she usually gets two a night) is seized with forepaw and carried in her mouth halfway around her tramway, to be torn into chewing-sized pieces on the corner shelf. The soft-boiled egg that is part of her meal several times a week is carefully held with both forepaws. She prefers to have a small hole made in the shell for her. Otherwise, sitting up on her haunches, she turns her head sideways and bites a piece out of the shell. Then her long, slender tongue, just made for extracting the soft yolk and then the white, goes into action. Phoebe doesn't stop licking until the shell is empty.

When the tropical-forest fruit crop is abundant, the arboreal feeding of kinkajous benefits animals on the ground. Agoutis, pacas, and tapirs depend upon the fruit the kinkajous drop.

In Panama, Phoebe ate fruits of the mamey tree. She relished the reddish pulp inside the brown sandpaper skin. Sometimes she fed so heavily that her *scats* were composed almost entirely of mamey pulp. During the summer she fed on the fleshy fruits of the slender-trunked trumpet tree. By fall, fruits of the alfaje were orange and ripe.

She also foraged among the canopy leaves of a large strangler fig. This curious tree, over 100 feet tall, had grown from a seed dropped by a fruit-eating bat. Lodged in a bark crevice, the seed sprouted and grew as an epiphyte on the host tree. It sent down aerial roots to extract moisture and minerals from the forest soil. Its leaves grew upward in search of sunlight. They soon overshadowed the host tree. In time, more and more roots encircled the trunk, eventually strangling the host tree. By Phoebe's time, the big strangler fig stood alone, supported by a hollow cylindrical trunk formed by the maze of its own roots. The strangler fig was a source of paired velvety green fruits that Phoebe found delicious.

Phoebe frequented wild nutmeg trees in search of their bitter-tasting two-part orange fruits. She relished the sweet, white-fleshed fruit of the animé tree. Sometimes she searched among the drooping branches of a spicy-smelling tree called the molenillo for round, buff-colored fruits, or climbed into a palm to feed from a large hanging cluster of fruits.

When a hog plum was heavily laden, she came to eat the sweet yellowish fruits. Almost nightly during the January-to-mid-March fruiting

58

season, she could be seen in a big almendro, foraging among its branches for brown-skinned fleshy green fruits.

Fruits for Phoebe in captivity are also seasonal. Bananas are the staple, and she likes them sliced, or at least with part of the peel laid back. She does not like citrus fruits, which is not surprising, since oranges are Old World trees. She tolerates apples and some canned fruits. She likes melons, watermelon most of all. She is most fond of fresh figs, available in some markets in late summer and fall and always expensive. Her food plate always includes fresh grapes: purple, red, or green. To savor their juice, Phoebe raises her head as she chews, or flops on one shoulder, turning her head upside down, or rolls onto her back to make sure none of the sweet liquid is lost.

Sugars are *carbohydrates* and good sources of energy. This may be why Phoebe likes to visit the kitchen. She knows the honeypot is kept there.

Phoebe hauls herself up onto a counter and crosses over the stove or takes the higher route, stepping carefully over and through a series of pots and pans on the shelf to reach the other counter. If someone has left a cabinet door ajar, Phoebe pries it open. Then she clambers up to the top shelf to rummage among the cans of baked beans, spaghetti, and tuna. She lets herself down to the next shelf, to find soups and canned fruits. She is not interested and drops lower. The bottom shelf offers edibles, at least some graham crackers in a box.

On the counter, Phoebe finds the honeypot, at last. Off comes the lid. Kinkajous are called "honey bears," and this is proof. Phoebe's long, thin tongue works in and out rapidly as she ingests the sweet, sticky liquid. Honey is better than marshmallows, or smelts, or even an egg!

Kinkajous are reported to have a fondness for alcoholic beverages. During a summer of fieldwork, Karl M. Waage, professor of geology at Yale University, made the acquaintance of a kinkajou in Taxco, Mexico. The kinkajou, on a leash, patrolled the bar top in the small mining town's cafe. Fascinated by a gentle-looking animal he had never before seen, Professor Waage approached for a closer look, only to be admonished by the barkeeper that the kinkajou might bite. There are several accounts of kinkajous that imbibed and soon after displayed a change of temperament, turning savagely on their keepers. Besotted, or just annoyed or enraged, a kinkajou, for all its docile appearance, can become a furry fury. Then curved claws become grappling hooks and fruit-eating teeth, especially the long canines, inflict deep puncture wounds.

In the tropical forest Phoebe found water in tree-crotch pools and on leaves. She almost never came down to drink. But when she hears water running, she sometimes leaves her room for a close-up look and feel. Unlike a raccoon, she never stays to dabble.

Phoebe and Physiology

Phoebe requires a warm-up period when she awakens. She prefers to lie quietly outside her basket before actively feeding or running about on her tramway. Sometimes, when the room temperature is below 70°F (22°C), her body shivers to increase metabolic heat production. With activity, her resting body temperature of 98.5°F (36°C) will rise to 101°F (38.5°C).

Phoebe, like other arboreal tropical mammals, has a low rate of basal metabolism. Basal metabolism, the heat produced while the animal is quiet, represents the minimum amount of energy necessary to maintain life at normal body temperature. Body size, as well as climate and feeding habits determine basal metabolism rates in animals and influence their energy expenditure. To maintain a constant body temperature, heat production must equal heat loss. *Metabolic rate* usually is measured by an animal's oxygen consumption.

Kinkajous, being tropical, are sensitive to extreme temperature changes. When excessive heat and humidity drive a kinkajou from its nest to drape on a branch and dangle bare-skinned palms and soles damp with sweat, its rapid breathing is apparent. If its body temperature reaches 101°F (38.5°C), the kinkajou begins to pant, drawing outside air over the moist mucous lining of nose and mouth. The panting is not dog-like. The kinkajou's mouth is only slightly open and its long, narrow tongue does not hang out or even protrude.

By sleeping in tree hollows or in shaded tangles, kinkajous avoid direct sunlight. If a sleeping place becomes too warm, a kinkajou is quick to move. Even so, dissipating, or getting rid of, body heat can be more of a problem than heat loss is. Experiments by two German physiologists suggest that periods of mild cold stress are better tolerated than exposures to high temperatures. After careful monitoring of body temperatures and oxygen intake of a kinkajou under laboratory conditions, they concluded:

> Through his thick fur, the ball-like resting posture and his ability to increase considerably the heat production, the kinkajou is hardly affected by ambient temperatures down to 5°C [just above 40°F]. In a hot environment, however, these little bears show signs of heat stress . . . at air temperatures above 33°C [90°F].*

*E. F. Müller and E. Kulzer, "Body temperature and oxygen uptake in the kinkajou," p. 162.

Phoebe has a coat of velvety plush. Soft, dense, and woolly, it is the kind of fur that sheds rain. Other tropical mammals have similar *pelage*—the spotted phalanger, or cuscus, a lemurlike possum of Australia, and three tree-living primates, the West African potto, the slow loris of southeast Asia, and the woolly monkey of South America. Even the okapi, the purplish-brown, striped-rump relative of the giraffe that lives in the Ituri Forest of Central Africa, has a plush coat. The little night monkey also has fur that is dense and woolly. Among arboreal mammals in South America, only the sloths, with long bristly coats, have better insulation than the kinkajou and the night monkey.

Reduced basal heat production is an energy-saving adaptation in the stable warm-and-moist climate of the tropical forest. The physiologists estimated that the kinkajou's lowered metabolic rate saves about 50 *KCals* per day.

A low rate of basal metabolism is common to mammals that have periodic food supplies. Kinkajous, being mobile, can move their feeding sites from tree to tree and probably travel considerable distances for foraging. But when there is widespread fruiting failure, food is scarce and they face a time of hunger. Then their low basal rate gives them an important energy-saving advantage.

Procyonids are adaptable animals. In the north, where winters are long and cold, snow is deep, and food is hard to find, raccoons den up. They prepare for this time of winter sleep by fattening during late summer and fall, when carbohydrate-containing foods are plentiful. Their bodies become padded with fat, a reserve that insulates and sustains them during winter, when cold and snow may keep them denned for days, weeks, or even several months.

It may be that the kinkajou's low rate of basal metabolism and the raccoon's ability to store fat and den for winter are parallel adaptations to the problem of seasonal food scarcity.

More About Kinkajous

Mating. Unlike the cubs of their coati relatives, whose weaning is timed to coincide with peak insect abundance, a cub can be born to a kinkajou at almost any time of year. This is because female kinkajous are polyestrous, or have more than one period of estrus (sexual receptivity) during the year.

At mating time the male sniffs and nips at the female's throat and lower jaw, apparently attracted by the secretions from her throat and mandibular glands. During the mating process he stimulates his mate by vigorously rubbing her sides. To do this he uses the insides of his wrists where an enlarged, pointed *radial sesamoid* bone is prominent. This bone nubbin, fur covered, can be felt on the inside of Phoebe's wrists. On a male's wrist the radial sesamoid is bare-skinned, presumably from wear. With greater enlargement and a rearrangement of muscles, this same small bone provides the giant panda with its unique bamboo-shoot-grasping "thumb."

Birth of a Cub. After a gestation of 98 to 115 days, relatively long for a small carnivore, a cub is born. The infant is sparsely covered with grayish hair over much of its tiny body. Its undersides are bare. Eyes and ears are tightly sealed.

At first the cub's world is one of warmth, touch, and smell. In the tree-hollow nursery den it sleeps, often in the snug wrap of its mother's tail, and suckles from one or the other of the two teats of her lower abdomen. The mother grooms and cleans her baby.

A mother kinkajou is protective. When alarmed she seizes her cub with a gentle mouth grip on the side of its small neck. With infant clinging upside down beneath her chest, she carries her baby to safety in the canopy.

Soon the cub's ears open. Like most dark-den babies, a kinkajou cub must wait two to three weeks more for its eyes to open. Meanwhile it crawls about in the den, bumbling on small spidery legs. It twitters and is reassured by the mother's chittering replies. In a week or two the cub hops about. Its tail, coiled at birth, has a reflexive grasp. But it is not until the end of the third month that the tail becomes fully prehensile. By then, the young kinkajou travels through the canopy with its mother, sampling fruits and insects to supplement her diminishing milk supply. Although weaning has begun, mother and cub will stay together for at least six months.

Der Maki mit der Wickelschwanze

Kinkajous are found from southern Mexico through Central America and South America, as far as the wooded plateau of Mato Grosso in Brazil. Kinkajou (or quincajou) is a French word, thought to be an interpretation-by-ear of the name used for this arboreal carnivore by the Tupi, native Brazilians who live along the Amazon River. The kinkajou is also known in South America as *el cuchumbi*.

For a time *el cuchumbi* was confused with another animal. The confusion became apparent in 1773 when a kinkajou was exhibited in Paris. The label on its cage read: *The kinkajou, animal unknown to all the naturalists*. Its place of origin was given as the "west coast of Africa." The confusion was compounded when the celebrated naturalist Georges Louis Leclerc, compte de Buffon, declared that in the West Indies there was an animal called the potto and that this animal was, in fact, the kinkajou.

Potto, however, is the name of a short-tailed West African primate that belongs to the loris family. Woolly-haired and about the same size and color as a kinkajou, the potto, like the kinkajou, spends its time in trees and feeds on fruits and insects. It is possible that slaves brought from West Africa to the Caribbean islands transferred the name of an animal they had known to a New World look-alike with somewhat similar habits.

71

A Final Word

Because of their honey-bear appearance and their usually gentle ways, kinkajous have often been kept in captivity. The French naturalist Baron Cuvier had correspondence with a M. Simon Chauveau, who lived with a kinkajou for many years. At one time, wrote M. Chauveau, he had thought of presenting his kinkajou to Cuvier, so that the famous scientist might see and observe a live kinkajou. But the kinkajou's gentle gestures and playful displays so delighted its owner that he never found the courage to part with it. On the third of January, 1780, the kinkajou died. A grieving M. Chauveau noted that it was his kinkajou's ninth winter in Paris, *"sans que le froid ni aucune autre chose eut paru l'avoir incommodé"* (without the cold or anything else seeming to have troubled it). The age of M. Chauveau's kinkajou is not known. But kinkajous in captivity tend to be long-lived. One kinkajou lived in the Amsterdam Zoo for 23 years and 7 months, a record span.

Phoebe is not a pet, in the usual sense that a dog or cat is a pet. Her ways are those of the wild and must be respected. She requires a room-sized place of her own with provision for some of the things a kinkajou likes to do and for places she likes to sleep. Her daily feeding involves careful preparation. And while her investigative ways result in far less havoc in the house than do those of an ever-curious raccoon, a kinkajou-at-large requires supervision.

74

Phoebe often goes to school. There she depends on me for climbing, hanging, and even for hiding.

Living with a kinkajou is an absorbing experience. According to Hans Kruuk, an ethologist who has studied hyenas in Africa and shared his living space with a hyena called Solomon, "there is no better way to get the 'feel' of the behavior of an animal than to have one constantly around the house."* We would agree. For having Phoebe around the house gives us the "feel" of the behavior of a kinkajou, a most unusual animal with most unusual ways.

*In Cynthia Moss, *Portraits in the Wild* (Chicago: University of Chicago Press, 1982), p. 299.

GLOSSARY

ADAPTATION: an inherited behavioral, structural, or functional characteristic that fits an animal (or plant) for its habitat

ARBOREAL: living in trees

BROMELIAD: a plant of the family Bromeliaceae, which includes the pineapple; many bromeliads grow as epiphytes in the tropical forest

CARBOHYDRATES: compounds of carbon with hydrogen and oxygen, such as sugars and starches, the primary sources of energy for animals

CARNIVORES: mammals that belong to the order Carnivora; also used to describe any flesh-eater

CIRCADIAN RHYTHM: a rhythm in behavior, metabolism, or some other activity that recurs about every 24 hours

COMMENSAL: an animal (or plant) of one species involved in a relationship with an animal (or plant) of another species, with one species benefited, the other neither benefited nor harmed

EPIPHYTE: air plant; a plant that grows on or is attached to another plant, but receives no sustenance from its host

ETHOLOGIST: one who studies animal behavior

FOLIVORE: an animal that eats leaves

FRUGIVORE: an animal that eats fruits

HABITAT: the living place of an animal (or plant)

HOME RANGE: the area over which an animal roams in the course of its normal activities

INVERSION: the act of being reversed, or turned in the opposite direction

KCAL: the amount of heat required to raise one kilogram of water one degree Centigrade

LIANA: a climbing woody vine, characteristic of tropical forests, that roots in soil but depends on a tree, or trees, for support

LOCOMOTE: move

LOCOMOTION: the act of moving, or being in motion

METABOLIC RATE: the speed at which an animal converts food into expended energy; a degree of activity at the biochemical level, usually measured by the animal's oxygen consumption

NOCTURNAL: active at night

OMNIVORE: an animal that eats both plant and animal foods

PALMIGRADE: a term used to describe a forepaw that is placed palm down; more spreading in shape and with fanlike arrangement of digits, a palmigrade forefoot has more mobility at the wrist than a digitigrade paw of dog or cat, which places the weight on the toes

PELAGE: the coat of a mammal, fur, hair, or wool

PHEROMONE: a substance released by an animal which affects the behavioral response of other animals of the same species

PLANTAR: pertaining to the sole of the hind foot

PREDATOR: an animal that kills other animals for its food

PREHENSILE: adapted for grasping and holding on

PREY: an animal that is captured for food by other animals

PROCYONIDS: members of the raccoon family, the Procyonidae

PROTEIN: organic compounds containing amino acids, the primary source of material for growth in animals

RADIAL SESAMOID: a small bone, present in some carnivores and sometimes enlarged, on the radial, or inner, side of the wrist

SCAPULA: shoulder blade

SCATS: an animal's feces, or droppings

SEBUM: the oily secretion of sebaceous skin glands

SEMIPLANTIGRADE: not quite flat-footed; only part of the plantar surface, or underside, of the foot contacts the ground or other surface

SUBTALAR JOINT: the moveable union of the talus and the calcaneus, bones of the ankle

TAPETUM: a light-reflecting layer of flattened cells behind the retina of the eye

TRANSVERSE TARSAL JOINT: the moveable union of calcaneus and talus (the two large bones of the ankle) and the smaller navicular and cuboid bones

REFERENCES

Ewer, R. F. *The Carnivores*. Ithaca, N.Y.: Cornell University Press, 1973.

Forsyth, Adrian, and Miyata, Ken. *Tropical Nature*. New York: Charles Scribner's Sons, 1984.

Janzen, Daniel H., ed. *Costa Rican Natural History*. Chicago: University of Chicago Press, 1983.

Jenkins, Farish A., Jr., and Deedra McClearn. "Mechanisms of hind foot reversal in climbing mammals." *Journal of Morphology* 182 (1984): 197–219.

Leigh, Egbert G., Jr., Rand, A. Stanley, and Windsor, Donald M., eds. *The Ecology of a Tropical Forest*. Seasonal Rhythms and Long-term Changes. Washington, D.C.: Smithsonian Institution Press, 1982.

McClearn, Deedra. "Morphological and behavioral adaptations for arboreality in the raccoon family, Procyonidae." *American Zoologist* 17 (1977): 975.

Müller, E. F., and Kulzer, E. "Body temperature and oxygen uptake in the kinkajou (*Potos flavus* Schreber), a nocturnal carnivore." *Archives Internationales de Physiologie et de Biochemie* 86 (1977): 153–163.

Poglayen-Neuwall, Ivo. "On the marking behavior of the kinkajou (*Potos flavus* Schreber)." *Zoologica* 51 (1967): 137–144.

Rensch, B., and Dücker, G. "Manipulierfähigkeit eines Wickelbären bei längeren Handlungsketten." *Zeitschrift fur Tierpsychologie* 26 (1969): 104–112.

Richards, Paul W. *The Life of the Jungle*. New York: McGraw-Hill Book Company, Inc., 1970.

ACKNOWLEDGMENTS

In the writing of a book about kinkajous in general, and Phoebe in particular, I relied on the help of innumerable people. There are some to whom I am especially indebted: To Deedra McClearn, of Harvard University, who gave us her Phoebe and, in generous support of a small project, permitted use of several photographs and discussed her work; to Ivo Poglayen, of the Reid Park Zoo, Tucson, Arizona, an authority on procyonids in general and kinkajous in particular, who responded to my queries about his and Inge Poglayen-Neuwall's experiences wth live-in kinkajous and provided photographs of baby kinkajous; to Richard G. Van Gelder, of the American Museum of Natural History, and Joseph A. Davis, of the Brookfield Zoo, mammalogists committed to carnivores, for sharing of ideas about procyonids; to Richard W. Thorington, Jr., of the Smithsonian Institution, for information about Barro Colorado, particularly the plant life on the island; to Peter Haller, of Eastchester, New York, ever-kind in helping with German translation; to Jennifer Haaser, who found a recent paper on kinkajou physiology in the course of her raccoon reading in Yale University's Kline Science Library; and to B. Elizabeth Horner, of Smith College, who took time from pursuit of her own research interests to record measurements and field notes on kinkajous in the collection of the Museum of Vertebrate Zoology at the University of California, Berkeley.

I would also thank Robert T. Orr, of the California Academy of Sciences, a keeper of some special mammals and a mentor for any mammalogist who writes.

A. H. Coleman, of the Museum of Comparative Zoology at Harvard University, fitted the preparation of a number of negatives and prints of Phoebe and her friends in Panama into his busy schedule. Farish A. Jenkins, Jr., kindly agreed to the use of artist Charles Gentry's pen-and-ink drawing of Phoebe pendant, which he owns.

For reminiscences and renditions of ''The Kinkajou'' and researching the sheet music in the library at Lincoln Center, I am grateful to Emily Cochran, my Hamden, Connecticut, neighbor.

Last but not least, my thanks go to Ellan Young, Phoebe's patient photographer; to Andy Young, her son and a superb animal photographer, who arranged for Phoebe to come to us; to Cope MacClintock, Margaret, and Pamela, who put up with Phoebe, as well as a wife and mother preoccupied with procyonids; and to Phoebe herself, with love.

DORCAS MACCLINTOCK

INDEX